Once Upon
A Time in
Caithness

Half-yokin' during the hay harvest at Cairnfield, Weydale, in 1948. (Submitted by W. Allan, Cairnfield).

Sergeant Harry Barrett dons an older style of uniform to welcome a re-enactment of the stage-coach journey from Inverness to Thurso. (Submitted by H. and M. Barrett, Thurso).

Once Upon A Time in Caithness

Compiled by
Clive Richards

Published by
North of Scotland
NEWSPAPERS
Wick, Caithness, Scotland

Acknowledgements

Many people have contributed to the making of 'Once Upon A Time' in Caithness.
The publishers acknowledge with gratitude the support, assistance and enthusiasm of the following without
whose co-operation this publication would not have been possible:
James Miller
Connie Gibbs

Grateful acknowledgement is made to the copyright photographs of:
Maurice Harrington
J. McDonald
Mario Luciani
UKAEA

Above all, a special tribute is made to Robert MacDonald of Northern Studios, Bridge Street, Wick,
Caithness whose photographs adorn the pages of this publication.

Finally, special thanks to the readers of the John O'Groat Journal and Caithness Courier who have responded to
our appeal for photographs of family, friends and memorable places and who have once again demonstrated the
true meaning of sharing.

A Catalogue Record for this book is available from The British Library.

ISBN 1 871704 33 2

Cover by Naver Limited, Thurso, Caithness.

Photocomposed by North of Scotland Newspapers, 42 Union Street, Wick, Caithness, Scotland.
Printed by Highland Printers, Henderson Road, Inverness, Scotland.

Introduction

Welcome to another selection of photographs from the old files of the John o'Groat Journal and the Caithness Courier, along with many sent in by readers. The story of Caithness over the last two centuries can be found in the albums and cupboards of the county.

We are very grateful to all the contributors who sent in so many interesting pictures that we had to make a selection from among them. The names of the individual contributors appear with the captions. All the unattributed pictures were taken by Robert MacDonald of Northern Studios who has been photographing Caithness life now for over thirty years.

In this look back at life in Caithness during mainly the 1970s - with the occasional glimpse further back or into the future - we can see some great changes taking place. This did not mean of course an end to the old ways, and the county continued to show, as it does to this day, a blend of continuity and innovation.

The pictures illustrate some key events, with some well-known faces putting in an appearance from time to time, as well as many of the special days in the county's year.

One long-term trend that has left its mark is increasing interaction with the south. Much of the old self-sufficiency has gone, symbolised most vividly by the incorporation of the county into the sprawling Highland Region in 1975.

Improvements to the A9 and the bridging of the Firths in Easter Ross have shortened the travel time south and a tendency to shop in Inverness has had its effect on local facilities. A similar trend on a more local scale has seen a movement of people from country to town or village with the resulting closure of some rural schools and the shrinking of kirk congregations.

Dounreay continues to be a major employer but the massive swing in public opinion from a pro- to an anti-nuclear stance has had its influence, and the reactor facility is now decommissioning. Smaller industries came and some went; and farming shifted and modernised. At the same time there has been a major decline in the fishing industry in Wick with severe economic consequences, but Scrabster began its ascent to become one of the top landing ports in the country.

The discovery of oil in the North Sea and, even more promisingly, only twelve miles off the east coast in the Beatrice Field brought great hopes for economic development, but these have not all been realised. A plan to build an oil-rig yard on Dunnet Beach came to naught, and there was talk at one time of oil-related developments in Murkle Bay.

The story goes on. Meanwhile, turn over these pages and enjoy a peedie trip down memory lane.

A shearing crew at Stemster Mains in the 1950s at the end of a long day's work.
(Submitted by C. Coghill, Georgemas).

Mary-Ann and James Calder, Westside, Dunnet. Pictured by their fireside in 1983. The cottage (Mary-Ann's Cottage) is now a museum. (Submitted by J. P. Campbell, Halkirk).

CONTENTS

On land and sea

Davie Steven, Puldagon, Stirkoke, taking a break while working as a ghillie for the Hornes of Stirkoke.
(Submitted by M. Hammerton, Hill of Forss).

Break for half-yokin' at Lieurary farm, possibly in the mid-1950s. (Submitted by C. Munro, Westerdale).

The Brims family at Lealands, Bilbster, in about 1910. (Submitted by J. and W. Coghill, Watten).

Angus and David Brims getting horses ready for showing. The picture was taken in the early 1900s.
(Submitted by J. and W. Coghill, Watten).

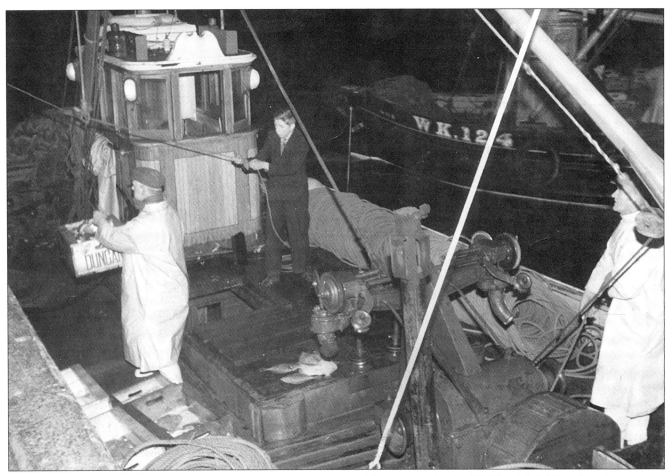

The *Harbinger* (WK96) unloading at Wick. Skipper Donald Miller at the winch with Hamish McLeod at the rope. (Submitted by Z. Sinclair, Wick).

The *Ebenezer* (WK135) in the early 1960s. (Submitted by Z. Sinclair, Wick).

Every autumn, Wickers joined the crowds of men and women from all along Scotland's east coast to work at the herring fishing in Yarmouth. These pictures were taken in about 1950. (Submitted by H. and P. Gray, Wick).

James Sinclair's kippering crew outside a dressing station run by the Church of Scotland. The picture was taken around 1949. The dressing stations provided the workers with elementary first aid and other facilities.
(Submitted by H. and P. Gray, Wick).

One of Wick's last herring drifters, the *Sweat Pea,* in drydock in the 1930s. (Submitted by H. and P. Gray, Wick).

A peaceful scene at Wick harbour in 1959.
(Submitted by M. Harrington, Thurso).

RNLI Inspectors visit the Thurso Lifeboat Station, April 1970.

Winter snow in 1955 at Jim Youngson's farm at Hoy, Olrig. The shepherd is James Manson. (Submitted by A. Manson, Thurso).

At the County Show, 1969. (Submitted by R. Campbell, Castletown).

Mrs Bremner picking seed potatoes from her tattie pit at Hill o' Wester in April, 1970.

Thurso Young Farmers' Club completed a ploughing marathon on 15th November, 1970, after turning over 128 acres of Scrabster Farm in four and a half days of non-stop driving. The drivers changed every four hours.

It looks as if six foxes were killed in this hunt at Wester Moss in May, 1970.

The *North Star* in Wick harbour, December, 1973.

Displenish sale of stock at Buckies farm, near Thurso, on 16th May, 1973. The sale was held by Hamilton's Auction Marts Ltd on behalf of Miss J. W. Davidson whose family had held a tenancy of the farm for some 300 years. All the livestock, machinery and implements realised high prices

The *Quo Vadis* joins the Wick white-fish fleet, August, 1975.

Stroma, 1975. Abandoned crofts.

One man – Mackie Banks of Canisbay, his dog, Mirk and a few sheep in the Latheron Agricultural Society sheepdog trials held at Nottingham Mains on 2nd August, 1986.

Stemster Mains, 1976, and staff receive clocks in recognition of their 25 years' service.
(Submitted by C. Coghill, Georgemas).

The 40-foot dual-purpose *Challenge*, here with skipper-owner George King at the wheel, at Scrabster in July 1986, was built from ferro-cement. (Submitted by M. Luciani, Thurso).

These fatted cattle of the Caithness farmland photographed in October, 1986 all belonged to crofter Peggy Mackay of Clashgall, Halkirk, who since 1972 had built up a herd of crossbreds that included many continental breeds.

The combined crews of the new 87-foot-long *Boy Andrew* (WK170), built for £1.2 million, and her namesake, renamed the *Opportune* (WK171), in Wick in June 1986. (Submitted by J. McDonald, Wick).

Skipper Ian Thomas at the helm of the *Pentland Venture* which took over the Groats-Burwick ferry from the *Souter's Lass* in May, 1987. Not long after her maiden voyage, the *Pentland Venture* played a role in the rescue of 21 people from the Bremerhaven trawler *Hessen* when the latter went down in the Pentland Firth, a life-saving effort that also involved two Sea King helicopters from HMS *Ark Royal*, fishing vessels and the Longhope lifeboat on the night of 25th June.

The *Fidelity* in 1913 became the first motor boat to operate from John O'Groats. (Submitted by K. Green, John O'Groats).

On 29th October, 1969, these two Ostend trawlers, the *Haai* and the *Massabielle,* were driven ashore at Thurso East. When the *Haai* fouled her propeller the *Massabielle* took her in tow. The manoeuvre broke down in heavy weather and one trawler dragged the other ashore. Two members of Thurso Sub-Aqua Club, George Gibson and William Stewart, played a key role in the rescue of the crews. (Submitted by A. Manson, Thurso).

The *Dora*, shown here at John O'Groats, was built in 1935 by two men from Stroma, Alfred Moir and Will Banks. (Submitted by K. Green, John O'Groats).

Dane Budge of Barns of Hempriggs, here with his wife, Carole, and their sons, Allan and Graeme, won the Bank of Scotland Ayrshire herd competition for remarkable dairy performance in 1988.

John Begg of the Commercial Hotel and Sheila Sinclair yarning at the County Agricultural Show at Braal, Halkirk, in 1983. (Submitted by J. P. Campbell, Halkirk).

Wilma Banks and Kim, from Gills, after winning the Parish championship, the Ladies Shield and the Intermediate Shield at the Mey sheepdog trials on 19th August, 1988.

Dr Jack Dunnet with a specimen of *Alhamra*, a Caithness-bred tattie that found popularity in Algeria. The picture was taken in February, 1989.

The ferry *Varagen* visits the pier at Gills Harbour at the end of July, 1989 during the preparations for the launch of the new service across the Pentland Firth.

The vehicle deck of the *Varagen* while she was moored at Gills.

A storm in the Pentland Firth, at the end of September, 1989, broke the linkspan.

Wick seiner *Ben Loyal* damaged her bows when she struck the wall at the entrance to the harbour in April, 1989. The fire brigade managed to save the vessel from sinking.

This century-old barometer, originally installed at Wick by the British Fisheries Society, was renovated at the Dounreay Apprentice Training Centre on behalf of the Wick Society and returned to the Wick Harbour Trust in February, 1989.

Intent faces at the old Hamilton's Mart beside the railway station in Thurso at a North Country Cheviot tup sale on 3rd September, 1976. (Submitted by L. Munro, Halkirk).

The *Golden Strand,* the latest addition to the Wick fleet in March, 1989.

Judging the North Country Cheviot two-shear tups at the Caithness Agricultural Society Show at Braal in 1983.
(Submitted by J. P. Campbell, Halkirk)

There is a timeless quality to these four shots of the Reay landscape. We don't know when they were taken or by whom, but we think it must have been in the early 1900s. The picture lower left is of the ruins of Dounreay Castle. (Submitted by E. Sutherland, Reay).

Northern Agricultural Executive Committee, May 1950: Back row, left to right: I. Stewart, D. M. Miller, G. Learmonth, R. Bruce, W. Bain, W. D. Munro. Front: J. M. Esslemont M.A., B.Sc (Agr) Senior Inspector, G. M. Nicolson, G. J. Grant, Vice-chairman, Brig. G.D.K. Murray, OBE, M.C., TD, A.D.C., DL, Chairman, Major G.C. Rutherford, CB, J.P., J.S. Banks, E.W. Ross, Assistant Secretary. Absent member: W. Spence.

Gala days

Ray Mackay, Wick's first post-war Herring Queen, steps ashore in July 1949 from the seiner *Royal Burgh* (WK 561). The event was a celebration of local enterprise and continuity, as the *Royal Burgh* was the latest boat from the yard of D.B. Alexander, and her skipper was William Shearer, whose daughter Rita had been the first Herring Queen back in 1937.

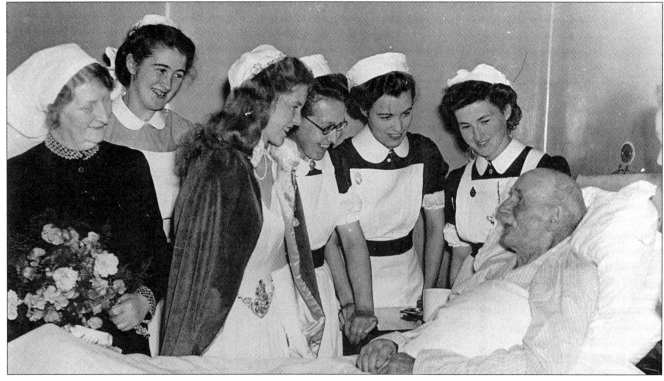

Ray Mackay exchanges kind words with a patient at the Bignold Hospital, Wick, in 1949. Left to right: Matron Bain, Nurse S. Leith, Ray Mackay, Sister M. Sutherland, Sister Forbes and Nurse T. Green.

All dressed up and here – waiting for the judges at the Thurso Gala in 1951. (Submitted by R. Campbell, Castletown).

The children's fancy dress parade at the Halkirk Gala, August, 1969.

The crowning of Castletown's Gala Queen, Kathleen Farmer, in June, 1969 accompanied by attendants, Barbara Graham and Kathleen Swanson.

A venerable form of transport re-appearing at Halkirk galas in the early 1970s. Left: William (Wink) Budge and Finlay Pauls. (Submitted by J. P. Campbell, Halkirk)

Halkirk Gala (approx 1970), John Begg on the vintage cycle – a star attraction.
(Submitted by J. P. Campbell, Halkirk).

Roy McKenzie and James Sutherland put in an appearance as the Steptoes at the Halkirk Gala, in about 1961.
(Submitted by M. Gunn, Halkirk).

Thurso's 1970 Gala Queen, Hilary Horne, is escorted from her coronation by
Provost T. W. Pollock.

The Rev. George Bell places the crown on the head of Canisbay's first mini-gala
Queen, Elizabeth Green, on 23rd July, 1970. According to the report in the *Groat*,
the community experienced its first barbecue on this occasion, with 'succulent
viands' and a Lassies v Loons football match.

The massed pipes and drums of bands from Wick, Thurso, Dornoch and Bonar Bridge in Thurso on 4th July, 1970.

The laughing policewoman – Mrs Peggy Barrett as a Highland bobby.
(Submitted by H. and M. Barrett, Thurso).

The fancy dress parade at Castletown Gala, 8th August, 1970.

More fancy dress shots from Halkirk Gala in the early 1970s. Alex Forbes keeps an eye on contestants as Andy Capp (Alistair Crawford) is kept in line by Flo (brother, Brian). (Submitted by J. P. Campbell, Halkirk).

Fancy dress, Halkirk Gala, around 1970/71 – Alexander Budge, Milton Farm, wishing he was home mucking out the byre. (Submitted by J.P. Campbell, Halkirk).

Nessie put in an appearance at Halkirk's gala on 15th August, 1970.

Provost Bill Mowat escorts Wick Gala Queen, Evelyn Miller, August 1968.

The crowning of Lybster's Gala Queen, Catherine Mackay, July 1968.

Scene from Lybster Gala procession, 1968.

Castletown Gala Queen, Elsa Swanson, gives her address, August, 1968.

A reunion of Gala Queens, for the years 1964 - 1974, at Castletown.

Colin Campbell, famous for his stand-up comedy based around local radio stations, entertains the Wick Gala Week crowd, 24th July, 1987. (Copyright J. McDonald, Wick).

Wick Gala Queen, Karen Cormack, with attendant Julie Miller, visit Deirdre Steven and son, Matthew, the first baby to be born in Caithness General Hospital during Gala Week, July 1987.

This sporting life

James Campbell on 'Danny Boy' won the open jumping competition at a County Show in the early 1960s.
(Submitted by R. Campbell, Castletown).

Halkirk Young Farmers 5-a-side football team 1958/59. Left to right: Donnie Gunn, David Allan, Ronald Mackenzie, John Finlayson and John Swanson.

The Halkirk small-bore rifle club in about 1957. (Submitted by J. P. Campbell, Halkirk).

Geoff Capes from Spalding, a frequent competitor in Highland Games, at the Halkirk Games in 1985 with Alastair Gunn. (Submitted by M. Gunn, Gerston).

The Halkirk teams won the Senior and the Junior Boys' Brigade League and were Cup Champions in 1975.
They remained unbeaten throughout the season.
Back row, left to right: R. Black, D. MacDonald, J. Paul, W. Mackay, G. Angus, J. Gunn, P. Blackwood. 3rd row: A. Gunn, S. Munro, P. Mackay, E. Sinclair, R. Omand, C. Elder, G. Macdonald. 2nd row: A. Crawford, K. Gunn, G. Andrew, A. Campbell, I. Campbell, I. Swanson, S. Blackwood. Front row: G. Paul, M. Forbes, G. Harper, S. Campbell. (Submitted by J. Gunn, Gerston).

Sarah-Ann Gunn leads the field on 'Salvador' at the County Show in 1984. (Submitted by M. Gunn, Gerston).

Her Majesty the Queen Mother talks to Charlie Simpson and Liam Gunn, captain of Halkirk Young Farmers, the winning tug o'war team at the Mey Games in 1990. (Submitted by M. Gunn, Gerston, copyright Northern Studios).

Young golfers at Wick Golf Club with instructor, David MacDonald, January, 1969.

The junior members of the Caithness Celtic Supporters' Club turned out in force at Bignold Park, Wick, on 10th July, 1970 to welcome a visit from player, Billy McNeill.

Thurso Swifts FC with their trophies from the 1946-47 season. (Submitted by R. Campbell, Castletown).

All eyes intent on the coach in this training session at Halkirk in about 1950. On the right stands headmaster, William Reid. Left to right: Coach (unknown), Donnie Allan, two obscured unknown, David Coghill, Ian Mackay, Donald Bruce, James Sutherland, Hamish Levack, Tom Munro, Ian Bruce, Pat Sutherland and Hugh Bain. (Submitted by J. P. Campbell, Halkirk).

The Halkirk team in the early 1960s. Back, left to right: Norman Mackenzie, John Campbell, Henry Ross, Pat Macleod, Jim Falconer, Acky Falconer, James Sclater, Ronald Mackenzie and George Mitchell. Front: Monty Sutherland, George Mackay, Lewis Sinclair, Donnie Mowat and Christy Cameron. (Submitted by J. P. Campbell, Halkirk).

The Castletown Ladies Darts team in the St. Clair Arms, December, 1972.

Lybster Portland FC, October, 1972.

The Halkirk Highland Games committee steps out on a sponsored walk in 1972.
Left to right: Will Gunn, John Porter, Peter Blackwood, Sandy Gunn, Bill Budge, Lord Thurso, Piper John MacRae,
Ronald Mackenzie, Jimmy Gunn and Peter Murchison.(Submitted by J. P. Campbell, Halkirk).

Wick Thistle FC, September 1968.

The Halkirk Youth Club football team, 1967. (Submitted by J. P. Campbell, Halkirk).

Sand yacht championships on Dunnet Beach, 2nd June, 1968.

Two members of the Wick Judo Club in action in the Assembly Rooms, 6th May, 1968.

Teams from the Halkirk Boys' Brigade and the 2nd Thurso Scouts competed in the final of the Courier Cup in Thurso on 18th March, 1970.

Some of the entrants in the Highland dancing festival at Mount Pleasant School, Thurso, in March, 1970.

Badminton trophy winners, 23rd March, 1973.

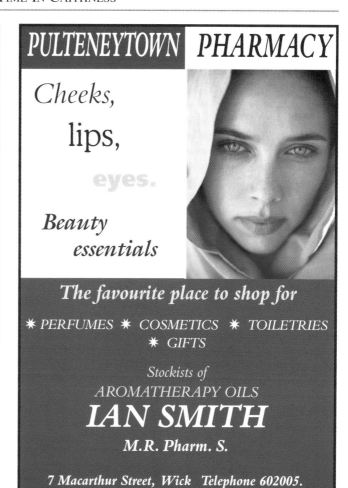
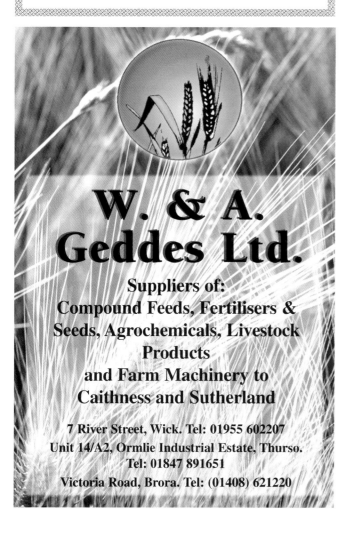

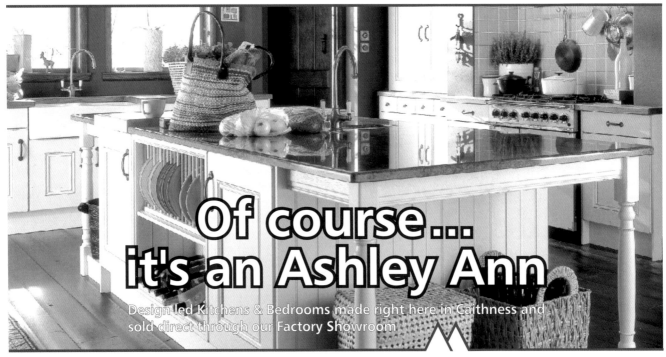

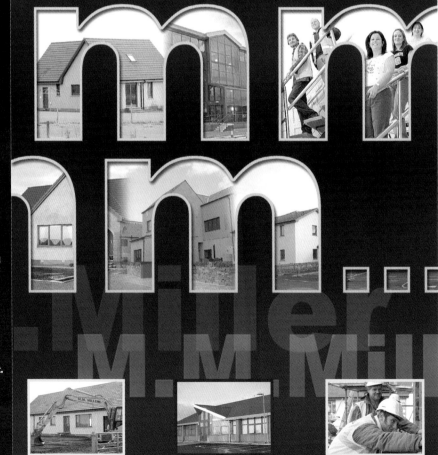

Fiona and Sinclair Bruce from Haster won the Stirkoke Rifle Club Young Scot trophy in March, 1973.

The Wick Cub Scouts football team, 22nd July, 1973.

Just for kicks? The second of a two-game tournament between football teams representing the licensees of Wick and Thurso took place in the Harmsworth Park on 12th August, 1973. On this occasion Wick won 6-4.

Wick Rugby Club won the County Trophy in September, 1973.

Members of Thurso Amateur Swimming Club at the Scottish finals, 15th September, 1973.

Wick Rovers FC, September, 1974.

A scorrie's eye view of the ring at Dunbeath Highland Games, July, 1974.

. . . . and a panorama of the landscape.

The 1975 trophy winners of Wick Golf Club.

Wick Groats FC, June 1975.

The opening of the 1975 season at the St. Fergus Bowling Club, Wick.

Lybster Golf Club trophy winners, 1977.

The ladies darts teams at the Commercial Hotel, Lybster, November, 1977.

Trophy winners of the Caithness Riding Club at the St. Clair Arms, Castletown, October, 1977.

Trophy winners at the Bower Rifle Club, May 1978.

Hugh Simpson Jnr won the Scottish Junior Championship of the National Small-bore Rifle Association in March, 1978.

The St. Clair Arms pub team, Castletown in about 1985. Back row, left to right: Alan Dunbar, Derek Oag, Terry Hossack, Banger Gunn, Graeme Campbell, Michael Macleod, Alan Swanson, Darkie Wares, Colin Hossack, Alan Gunn. Front row, left to right: Stuart Campbell, Graeme Macdonald, Lachie Sutherland, Alan Mowat, Will Farmer. (Submitted by R. Campbell, Castletown).

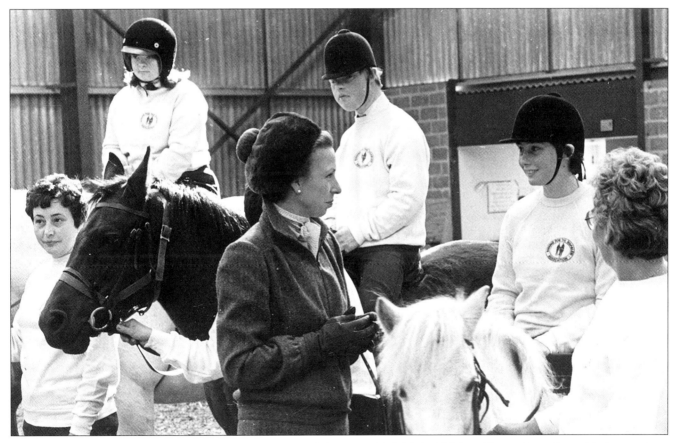

HRH Princess Anne visits the Riding for the Disabled Centre at Halkirk in 1984 and has a short chat with Annmarie Dunnett, Canisbay, one of the members of the riding team who put on a display during her visit to the Halkirk centre. Also in the photograph are two other members of the team, Lorraine Macgregor, Milton and Clive Mappin, Watten, along with helpers, Mrs Liz Gunn (left) and Mrs Marie Falconer, both Halkirk.

In June 1987, Ken Nicol, secretary of the Pentland Canoe Club, received an award from councillor John Green, chairman of the Caithness District Council environmental health committee, in recognition of the Club's four-year effort to clear litter from beaches at Dunnet, Reay and Thurso.

Derek Youngson (left) and David Barnes (centre) set a new record for the crossing of the Pentland Firth when they water-skied from Gills to Burwick and back in 49 minutes 2 seconds during the Gills Harbour Association gala on 5th July, 1987. Here councillor Bill Mowat presents them with trophies in recognition of their feat.

Roy Mackenzie and Pradip Datta, runner-up and winner respectively of the Forest Homes League trophy, receive their prizes from Mrs Carolanne Morrison at Wick Squash Club, May, 1988.

A husky team goes through its paces at the Forss Show in June 1989.

The Forss Show also staged an 'It's a Knock-out' competition that included this game in which the contestant had to cross between two trailers on a narrow beam and avoid being knocked off by a swinging bag.

The *Groat's* football correspondent, Iain Grant, presents the John O'Groat Journal County League trophy to Colin MacLeod, captain of the Castletown team, in July 1989.

A few of the members of the Pentland Rifle Club which celebrated its Diamond Jubilee in January, 1970.

A badminton team in Castletown in about 1978. (Submitted by R. Campbell, Castletown).

The Ladies Committee of the Halkirk Highland Games. (Submitted by J. P. Campbell).

Caithness at work

The men of Pulteney Distillery in 1922. Back row, left to right: J. Robertson, manager, Mr Douglas, Excise, D. Fraser, general, D. Steven, carter, D. Swanson, tun room, W. Farquhar, maltman, H. Gunn, tun room, Mr Brown, Excise. Front row: A. Polson, brewer, D. Hendry, maltman, D. More, cooper, W. Coghill, stillman, D. Bain, cooper, Mr Pollard, Customs Surveyor; overnight shift (not in picture) J. Gunn, stillman, J. Clyne, maltman.

High Street being widened in Wick in 1971, and the disappearance of many familiar shops. (Submitted by Z. Sinclair, Wick).

Summer 1960, and workmen from D.M. Geddes and Sons, and Alex Sutherland's take a break from dealing with the aftermath of a fire at John O'Groats House Hotel. Back row, left to right: W. Kerr, J. Falconer, S. Bain, D. Doull, G. Douglas, D. Calder, R. McCarthy. Front row: J. Manson, D. McKay, D. Geddes. (Submitted by A. Manson, Thurso).

The Harrow flagstone works around the year 1900. (Submitted by M. Gunn, Gerston).

John Miller (centre) and his staff outside his joiner shop in Halkirk in the 1920s. Left to right: Dan Simpson, Donnie MacDonald, John Miller (owner), Har Robertson, Gordon Steven and unknown. (Submitted by J. P. Campbell).

The premises later became those of Alexander Auld – ironmonger, building contractor, radio, TV and electrical engineers. The Auld brothers (Alexander, front left and George, front right) are pictured here with the staff in the early 1960s. Back, left to right: Alan Spencer, John Swanson, Peter Malcolm, John Begg, Sandy Campbell, Willie John Bain, Hugh Sutherland, Dougie Cameron, Tommy Bain, George Sutherland, Jimmy Bain, George Moodie and Charlie Jones. Sheena MacDonald is seated between the brothers. (Submitted by J. P. Campbell).

The bowler-hatted George Heggie, the head gardener at Barrogill Castle (Castle of Mey), with his staff at the beginning of the 20th century. (M. Gunn, Gerston).

Dr D.W.R.N. Sutherland is the principal guest of the opening of Mark Templeman's glove factory in Sinclair Street, Thurso, on 26th June, 1970.

In June 1970 when Sutherlands of Wick set off with a consignment of goods for a destination by Lake Constance on the Swiss border, such foreign trips were rare.

On 19th September, 1970, a large transformer for the PFR at Dounreay was carried through Thurso after being landed from a ship in Wick.

On 30th September, 1970, HRH Princess Alexandra signs the visitors' book in the Town Hall, after naming Wick's new lifeboat the *Princess Marina*.

At work in Thurso brick factory, November, 1972.

Cutting stone in A & D Sutherland's workshops at Spittal Quarry, January, 1970.

Salmon netting at Crosskirk Bay, August, 1974.

Trucks of GECO (UK) were commissioned by London-based firm Industrial Scotland Energy to carry out seismic surveys for possible oil deposits in much of west and central Caithness, October, 1986.

Alexander Bell, the Reporter for the public inquiry held at Thurso Town Hall in April 1986 into the siting of the European Demonstration Reprocessing Plant, visits Dounreay to see reprocessing at first hand. Opinion in Caithness on the EDRP was sharply divided, and the debate was fuelled by the Chernobyl disaster in Ukraine in May and the revelation that a leukaemia cluster had existed in the Thurso area between 1979 and 1983. The Thurso inquiry ended in November, after setting a record of 95 days for the longest and costliest in Scottish history. UKAEA and British Nuclear Fuels Ltd were eventually given the green light to build the EDRP but changes in nuclear policy in Europe made the decision redundant. (Copyright UKAEA.)

John Humphries published many books on local themes under his imprint of Caithness Books from his small press in Thurso. When this picture was taken in December 1986 he was about to start printing books for Kenyan schools with the help of a grant from Thurso Rotary Club

The bakery staff of the Co-op Bakery, Macrae Street, Wick, snapped in 1960. From left, Ian Sutherland, apprentice, Donald Anderson, foreman, Isobel Davidson, despatch worker, Alistair Robertson, baker.
Photo taken by Raymond G. Macdonald, baker.

A Leyland double-decker that carried workers to and from Dounreay during construction in the 1950s.
(Submitted by W. Sutherland, Thurso).

This Albion six-wheeler was also part of the bus fleet serving the Dounreay workforce in the 1950s.
(Submitted by W. Sutherland, Thurso).

Early days of Caithness aviation. Greta Green and Nan Manson beside an aircraft of E. L. Gandar Dower's Aberdeen Airways at the Claredon landing strip outside Thurso, in the 1930s. There was great rivalry between Aberdeen Airways and Highland Airways, run by Captain E.E. Fresson. (Submitted by W. Sutherland, Thurso).

The bridge by-pass at Dunbeath under construction in the summer of 1989.

Alistair and Iain Sutherland founded Caithness Peat products to market milled peat to gardeners in 1989.

Iain Robertson, chief executive of Highlands and Islands Enterprise, uses a glass trowel to break the sod for the construction of Caithness Glass's new factory at Wick Airport on 1st May, 2001. Looking on are Caithness Glass director, Matt Young and CASE chief executive, Don Clarkson.

This lorry with a load of carrier pipes for the Rockwater flowline bundle construction facility at Wester was one of several that had to inch their way through Wick in the summer of 1991.

Well known Caithness bobby, Jimmy Greig (second right), helps stretcher a casualty during Operation Snowdrop. (Submitted by his son, Jim Greig, Thurso).

Let's have a party!

Caithness five years old and under in the Wick Old Parish Church beginners class of the Sunday School, taken just before the Second World War. (Submitted by H. and M. Barrett, Thurso).

A Farmers' Ball in the 1920s? (Submitted by H. and M. Barrett, Thurso)

The end-of-term dance for Dora Miller's night-school sewing class for 1938-39. (Submitted by H. and M. Barrett, Thurso).

A wedding in the Breadalbane Hall, Wick, possibly in the 1930s. (H. and M. Barrett, Thurso).

The Ideal Dance Band against a backdrop of Keiss Castle on an unknown date some time in the 1930s or 1940s.
Left to right: Billy Gray, Willie Nichol, Bob Edwards, George Cormack, Sandy (Matt) Matheson, Ella Bean, W. More.
(Submitted by J. Gunn, Wick).

The Ideal Band again. (Submitted by R. Taylor, Wick).

The Imperial Dance Band performing in the Breadalbane Hall some time after the end of the Second World War. (Submitted by Z. Sinclair, Wick).

A Thurso Swifts dinner dance in the 1950s. (Submitted by R. Campbell, Castletown).

The Woolworths staff dance, Wick, at some time during the 1950s.
(Submitted by M. Harrington, Thurso, copyright J. McDonald).

Some of the guests at what we think was a WRI supper at the Ross Institute, Halkirk, in 1958 or 1959.
Left to right: Lena and Dod Swanson, Willie and Johan Lyall, Cath Jack and Will Sclater (extreme right). The young
lad in front of the table is Hamish Lyall. (Submitted by J. P. Campbell, Halkirk).

The Caithness Badminton Club dinner dance in 1980. (Submitted by R. Campbell, Castletown).

A Caithness Farmers' Ball in the mid-1950s. (Submitted by M. Gunn, Gerston).

We think the Wick bride-to-be getting some special attention in this picture is Barbara Bean who was married in September, 1939. (Submitted by H. and M. Barrett, Thurso).

Pupils at Wick North School in the 1920s. (Submitted by H. and M. Barrett, Thurso).

Ethel Jack and the pupils of Mey School with the Christmas cake gifted by Her Majesty the Queen Mother each year.
The picture was taken in 1959 or 1960. (Submitted by H. and M. Barrett, Thurso).

The Wick Variety Dance Band playing at a wedding reception in the Nethercliffe Hotel, Wick, in 1958.
(Submitted by Mackay, Wick).

The London Caithness Association dinner on 6th November, 1953.
Mr Bruce, Miss Harmsworth, Mr Harmsworth, Miss Bruce, Hon. Robin Sinclair, Hon. Catherine Sinclair, G.C.D.D. President, Sir Richard Dunbar, Lord Reay,
Mrs Harmsworth, Mr Marlow, Lady Robertson, Sir David Robertson M.P. (Submitted by Sir Richard Dunbar).

Wick Hairdressers' dinner dance, Christmas 1969.

The Debonaires Dance Band ready for the road, March, 1969.

The Debonaires at Wick harbour. Left to right: Johnny Polson, Stanley MacNab, Hamish Duncan, Adam Polson, Marcelle Robertson and Willie Byrne. (Submitted by R. Byrne, Wick).

Willie Byrne also played in the Midas Touch, here snapped in the seventies. (Submitted by R. Byrne, Wick).

Three other bands of the 1960s, the Falcons . . .
(Submitted by C. Byrne, Wick, copyright Harrington).

. . . the Newmen. (Submitted by R. Byrne, Wick).

. . . and the Rhythm Four, pictured here with Tommy Gemmell and Bertie Auld (2nd and 3rd from left behind) at a Celtic Supporters Club dinner dance. Rest of line-up from left is: Andrew Sinclair, unknown, Heather Mackay, Richard Begg, Jim McKenzie, Sandy Chisolm and Sandy Green. (Submitted by C. Byrne, Wick).

Willie Byrne and Catherine McCaughey at their wedding in Wick Old Parish Church, 25th June, 1965. (Submitted by R. Byrne, Wick).

This group of revellers at the Farmers Ball in the Royal Hotel, Thurso in the 1960s look as if they have been giving the photographer a hard time. (Submitted by M. Harrington, Thurso).

Another Farmers Ball, this time in February, 1961, with a slightly more attentive crowd.
(Submitted by M. Harrington, Thurso).

The first-year Christmas party at Wick High School, 1972.

Three entrants in the 1970 attempt at Canisbay to break the marathon dance record for Britain. At the event, run to aid the funds of Canisbay Youth Club and Pentland United Football Club, 54 competitors began dancing on the evening of Friday, 18th May. The last dancer, Alistair Manson from Lower Gills, survived until one o'clock on Tuesday morning, after 61 hours, beating the previous record of 56 hours.

Merry revellers at a Christmas party thought to have been held at the Dounreay Control Tower, possibly in 1960. The group includes staff from Langdon and Every, a quantity surveying firm and UKAEA. (A. Fraser, Dounreay Communications; photo belongs to Isobel Donnelly, Thurso).

The Tufty Club Christmas Party in Wick Assembly Rooms, 1972.

The dinner dance of Caithness Field Club, November, 1972.

Keiss Football Club at their presentation dinner in the Seaview Hotel, John O'Groats, September, 1968.

The Thurso Scout Group dinner dance at the Seaview Hotel, John O'Groats, 12th January, 1973.

Castletown Friendship Club party, January, 1973.

Caithness Coastguards enjoy their dinner dance at John O'Groats on 2nd March, 1973.

The Wick Christian Endeavour Band, March, 1973.

Fashion show organised on 4th April, 1973 by the Caithness branch of the British Diabetic Association in the Wick Assembly Rooms.

Many former residents of Stroma with their families and friends got together for this reunion in the Seaview Hotel, John O'Groats on 27th July, 1973.

The 5th Battalion of the Seaforth Highlanders hold their reunion in Mackay's Hotel, Wick, on 2nd August, 1974.

It's not every party that's graced by two horses, but this was the scene at the Christmas dance for the staff of the three Wick hospitals on 19th December, 1975.

Taking time off from their sums, Wick Inland Revenue staff celebrate Christmas, December, 1975.

Murkle Children's Committee dinner dance, 5th December, 1975.

Wick Accordion and Fiddle Club in Mackay's Hotel in the winter of 1989.

Thurso magician, June Leith, and Lybster puppeteer, Keith de Paola, entertain youngsters in the Wick Scout Hall on April Fool's Day, 1989.

Memories are made of these

The old poor-house at Latheronwheel.

Wick North School, 1910. The teacher is Miss Kate Budge.

Teacher Miss Kate Budge. Top row, left to right: Jimmy Coghill, Donnie Miller, George Falconer, Sandy Dunnet, Peter Wilson, Pheenie Miller, Jimmy Dunnet, George Munroe, Johnnie Sinclair. Second row: Sandy Steven, Jimmy Malcolm, Tommy Buchanan, David Leith, Angus McDonald, Willie Huston, Alex Thain, John Ross, Ackie Gray, Hamish Wilson, Francie Coghill, David McGregor. Third row: Maggie Beatie, Jessie Gunn, Mary Ann Durrand, Jessie McLeod, Margaret Manson, Georgina Smith, Katie Munroe, Ina Malcolm, Maggie McGregor, Georgina Sutherland, Annie Farquhar. Fourth row: Johan Harper, Sybell Davidson, Bella Leith, Lissie Miller, Maggie Muir, Mennie Rosie, Jessie Gray, Dolly Turner, Maggie Jane Melville, Alice Mcleod. Bottom row: George Cormack, Jimmy McAdie, John George Steven, Donald Williamson, David McAdie, Eddie McDonald, David McGregor, Finlay Sutherland, John Bain.

(Submitted by J. Gunn, Wick).

A procession along Bridge Street, Wick, in June 1911, to celebrate the coronation of King George V.
(Submitted by C. Coghill, Georgemas).

The junction of Dempster Street with the main road south out of Wick was always prone to flooding, as on this occasion on 12th November, 1909. The old West Church stood where Dunnet's garage is now.
(Submitted by C. Coghill, Georgemas).

Another coronation celebration, this time in 1953 at Stemster House.

Bonfire on Harpsdale Hill, Coronation celebration. From the top are Jake Mackay, Will Gunn, Jake Waters, Peter Campbell, unknown, David Andrew (Strath), unknown, Davey Swanson, unknown, Jackie Miller, Alex Wares, Dave Wares, Dave Andrew (Achies), unknown. (Submitted by J. P. Campbell, Halkirk).

111

They don't make them like this anymore – Jessie Mackay at the wheel at Rattar Mains in about 1935. (Submitted by M. Gunn, Halkirk).

1945 – and the Caithness Battalion of the Home Guard parade through Wick. (Submitted by RBLS Club, Thurso).

The Lybster section of the 5th Seaforths at the TA camp in 1913 (RBLS Club, Thurso).
Back row, left to right: Not known, not known, D. Bain, J. Gunn, JAS Duncan, Sutherland, A. McKenzie (killed in action), Jas Sinclair. Front: J. Cormack, W. Gunn, D. Sutherland, G. Cormack.

The first charabanc at John O'Groats Hotel arrived in about 1920. Ivy Sinclair, late of Ormlie Hall, Thurso in front, Jack, Jim and Ada Laird with Ivy Sinclair, grandchildren of Mrs Calder who had the hotel.
(Submitted by Kathleen Green, Roadside, John O'Groats).

Wendy Levett, personifying the Spirit of 1951, delighted the audience at Wick's annual Old New Year Party in the Breadalbane Hall, on 31st January, 1951. The event had been held later than usual because of a 'flu epidemic'.

We think this is a picture of pupils at Latheron school in the 1930s.
(Submitted by J. Murrison, Latheronwheel).

114

A smart turn-out at Watten school in 1937. (Submitted by J. and W. Coghill, Watten).

The members of the Celtic embroidery class run by the Dunbeath WRI - in the 1930s? - show off their handiwork.
Back row, left to right: Lil McKay, Dunbeath, Minnie Keith. Front: Dunbeath boy, E. McKenzie, C. Barnie, Dunbeath,
Mrs Joe McKay, Dunbeath, Pearl Doull, Mrs J. Cormack, Dunbeath boy.
(Submitted by J. Murrison, Latheronwheel).

Latheron School, 1937 (Submitted by J. Murrison, Latheronwheel).

Wick High School pupils in the 1950s, we think. (Submitted by J. Murrison, Latheronwheel).

Alex Matheson, pictured here in 1991, was the last carter plying for hire in Caithness. Alex and his father, Will, worked their trade for 120 years in all. (Adams pic submitted by Matheson, Fearn).

Willowbank, Wick in 1954. Although there was a BP garage in the foreground, there was not a car to be seen in the street. They were probably all glued to the box as the aerial on the first chimney confirms the arrival of TV.

The Caithness Air Raid Police during the Second World War. (Submitted by M. Harrington, Thurso).

Checking tyre pressure at Macrae and Dick's garage in Whitechapel Road, Wick in the mid-1950s.
(Submitted by Miller, West Lothian).

Wick High School in 1946. (Submitted by W. Coghill, Watten).

Lybster Brownies and Girl Guides in the 1950s (Submitted by J. Murrison, Latheronwheel).

Halkirk Guides, 1948-49. Back row, left to right: Norna Pottinger, Joey Henderson, Margaret Shearsmith, Nellie Swanson, Anne Mackenzie, Nettie Polson, Isobel Campbell, Margaret Swanson, Jenny Oliver. Middle: Nancy Wares, Anne Henderson, Margaret Polson, Isobel Macdonald, Isobel Campbell, Christine Wares, Eleanor Scott, Elma Gunn, Elizabeth Mackenzie, Isobel Pottinger. Front: Catherine Sutherland, Miss Nan Davidson, Margaret Murray and Anne Lyall. (Submitted by J. P. Campbell, Halkirk).

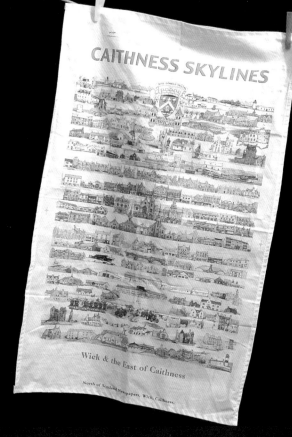

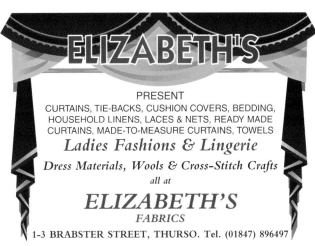

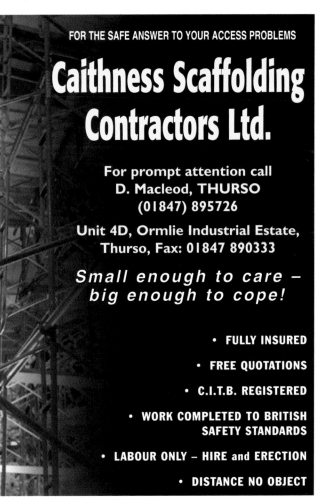

Wick Girl Guides in the late 1950s. Back row, left to right: Marcella Swanson, Marwin Muir, Elizabeth Sutherland, Myra ???, Susan Dunnett, Geraldine Robertson, Agnes Nicol, Mina Stewart, Betty Smith, Maisie Mackenzie, Lynne McKain, Margaret Gunn. Girl Guide leaders: Anne Dunnett, Jane Begg, Isobel Milne, Catherine Simpson. Middle row: Evelyn Cormack, Barbara Webster, Jennifer Sinclair, Margaret Gunn, Christine Meiklejohn, Elizabeth Ann Watt, Yvonne Smith, Louise Meiklejohn, Mary Gunn, Margaret Sutherland, Patsy Grant, Carole Eaton, Marion Maclean, Elizabeth Shearer, Mario Godziszko. Front row: Margaret Budge, Helen Sinclair, Patsy Wares, Evelyn Harness, Margaret Calder, Kay Henderson, Eileen Anderson, Jeanette Durrand, Marlene Steven, Janet Sutherland, Jean Baikie, Mary Gunn. (Submitted by Evelyn Miller, Elgin).

Tannach School in the late 1920s. (Submitted by M. Hammerton, Hill of Forss).

Wick Girls' Pipe Band changing formation in quick time at the Riverside in August, 1953.
(Submitted by H. and M. Barratt, Thurso).

Wick North School, then situated in Girnigoe Street, won the Junior Choir Trophy in 1925. Then are seen here with their teacher, Mrs Eadie. The adjudicator was Hugh Robertson, the famous choirmaster who led the Orpheus Choir.
(Submitted by H. and M. Barrett, Thurso)

122

The pupils of South School, Wick, in the mid-1950s.
Back row, left to right: Otto Matheson, Ernest Bremner, not known, George Bain, George Bremner, Alex Newlands, not known, Neil Groat, James Gray, Alie Williamson. Middle: Zena Sinclair, Jane Sinclair, Marwin Bremner, Kay Price, not known, Jeanette Shearer, Kay Henderson, Georgina Alexander, Dorothy Davidson, not known, Rosleen Mathieson, Yvonne Hodgson. Front: Donald MacPhee, not known, Margaret Sutherland, Nancy Anderson, Wilma Mackenzie, not known, Sandra Robertson, Rosalind Falconer, Jim Patmore, Alex Macleod.
(Submitted by Z. Sinclair, Wick).

Pupils at Wick North School in the 1950s.
Top row, left to right: James Dawson, Sandy Green, Ian Robertson, George Weir, Robert Adamson, John Maleham, Harry Gray, George Taylor, James Smart, Donald Leith, D. Harper. Centre: James Sutherland, Kenneth McVey, Ray Coghill, Margaret T. Bruce, Margaret MacPhee, Alison Banks, Kathleen Glass, Hazel Durrand, Patricia Meiklejohn, Margaret Fraser, Isobel Sutherland, Hope Easson, Jean Mackenzie, Irene Beattie, Ronnie Mackay, Alan Sutherland, Rodk. Gunn. Bottom row: Eric Farquhar, Sandra McNeal, Rosemary Anstey, Catherine More, Francis Neilson, Norma Macleod, Jean Geddes, Vida Shearer, Catherine Roy, Rosaline Lyall, Doris Durrand, Maria Dunnet, Christine Henderson, Alastair Steven, Robert Macdonald.
(Submitted by M. Harrington, Thurso).

Top row, left to right: Joe Sinclair, Wm Miller, Billy Bremner, Pat Mackay, D. Sinclair, R. Macbeth, Ian Macdonald, Ian Nicol, Donald Munro, Ian Bruce, Archie Macdonald. Centre: J. Henderson, John Ross, Victor Watson, I. Sutherland, B. Bruce, M. Sinclair, Lilian Coghill, Kathleen Innes, June Begg, Margaret Maclean, Elizabeth Mackay, Audrey Durrand, Norma MacGregor, Donald Farquhar, Andrew Miller, Marcus Taylor, Hamish Clark. Bottom: Nancy Durrand, Cath Henderson, I. Davidson, Nanette Gall, Isobel Leith, Patricia Mackie, Nina Clyne, Lil Gunn, Jean McGillivary, Janet Anderson, Jenny Banks, Mina Harper, Jenny Mitchell, Donald Bruce.
(Submitted by M. & M. S. Harrington).

Class VIA at Pulteneytown Academy, 1957. The teacher is Miss Christine Mackay. Back row, left to right: James Miller, William Mackay, David Henderson, Bryon Harness, Ronald Aitkenhead, Ian Kirk, Kenneth Farmer, Norman Macleod, Raymond Durrand. 3rd row: Ann Lyall, Yvonne Smith, Wilma McKain, Roberta Williamson, Margaret Skinner, Elizabeth Sutherland, Elizabeth Sinclair, Geraldine Robertson, Kathryn Torne. 2nd row: Grace Mackay, Joan Raspin, Christine Malcolm, Catherine Harper, Cecilia Macdonald, Patricia Farmer, Norma Webster, Eileen Anderson, Frances Baikie, Zena Sinclair. Front: James Durrand, Alan Stubbings, John Swanson, Richard Miller, Ian Mackenzie.
(Submitted by Z. Sinclair, Wick).

St. Fergus Inn, High Street, Wick, clearly in the days before Wick voted to go dry.
(Submitted by C. Byrne, Wick).

Bridge Street, Wick, bathed in sunshine on a winter morning, probably some time in the 1950s. (Submitted by H. and M. Barrett, Thurso).

125

George Bain, for many years local manager for British European Airways. The picture was taken in 1965.
(Submitted by Z. Sinclair, Wick).

The members of the Eastern Star in about 1948. (Submitted by H. and P. Gray, Wick).

Halkirk Cubs in 1958-59 with their leader, Joey Lennie. Back row, left to right: Charlie Miller, Kenneth Cameron, Billy Spencer, John Sclater, Gordon Spencer, John Sinclair, George Cameron, Adam Ross, James Campbell, Hugh Mackay, Sandy Bremner, Hamish Lyall, unknown at back and Willie Manson. Front: Grant Macdonald, John Mackenzie, Richard Bremner, Ian Banks, Bryan Horne and Leslie Bremner. (Submitted by J. P. Campbell, Halkirk).

The Halkirk Scouts - in uniform in 1956-57. Back, left to right: Ronald Mackenzie, Gordon Watt, Donald Mackie, John Campbell, John Macpherson. Second row: David Manson, Monty Sutherland, George Moodie, Hugh Mackay and Billy Gunn. Third row: Will Kennedy, Donnie Munro, Alex Mowat, George Sutherland and Calder Bain. Front: Christy Cameron, Stewart Manson, John Omand, Lindsay Crosby, not known, David Sutherland. (Submitted by J. P. Campbell, Halkirk).

. . . and having a party in the following year, 1957-58. Back two rows, left to right: George Sutherland, John Omand, unknown, Isobel Kennedy, Ishbel Harper, Ronald Mackenzie, Will Kennedy, Christine Polson, John Macpherson, Stewart Manson, David Manson, Pauline Crosby, Billy Gunn, Alistair Gunn, Anne Polson, David Sutherland, Donnie Munro, Donnie Macdonald, Nancy Campbell and Kathleen Farmer. Front: Jean Ross, Alec Miller, Mary Crosby, Barbara Crowden and Ian Sell. (Submitted by J. P. Campbell).

The 1st Wick Company of the Boys' Brigade in their centenary year, 1987. (Submitted by H. and P. Gray, Wick).

The 1st Thurso Company of the Boys' Brigade included a display of gymnastics in their variety concert in Thurso Town Hall on 25th March, 1970.

Scottish country dance winners with Mrs Gallon at Thurso High School in the early 1960s.
(Submitted by H. and M. Barrett, Thurso).

129

Easter bonnets on parade at Wick Old Parish Church, perhaps in 1982.
(Submitted by H. and P. Gray, Wick).

Watten WRI celebrate their golden jubilee in 1982 in the Pentland Hotel, Thurso.
(Submitted by S. Waters, West Watten).

Jim Campbell with the Co-op grocery and butcher van in the mid-1950s.
(Submitted by R. Campbell, Castletown).

A presentation dinner of Sinclair's Mart, Wick, in 1963. (Submitted by C. Coghill, Georgemas).

The Founder Committee members of the Thurso Royal British Legion. (Submitted by RBLS, Thurso).

Caithness students kidnapped Pearl Murray, the Press and Journal women's editor, outside the Thurso Youth Club during the Aberdeen University charities campaign, March 1969.

Wick TA Hall was struck by fire on 23rd April, 1969.

The first meeting of the Killimster WRI on 27th March, 1969.

The Thurso Players in rehearsal for the SCDA One-Act Festival in February, 1970.

A scramble for bargains at Thurso West Church sale of work on 30th April, 1970.

Bethy Munro presents
Lady Thurso with a gift at the
opening ceremony for Halkirk
bridge in November, 1970.
(Submitted by J. P. Campbell,
Halkirk).

Thurso Floral Art Club celebrates its first birthday at the Technical College, 25th June, 1970.

Thurso Rotary Club sponsored the building of this viewpoint indicator on Victoria Walk, Thurso in June, 1970.

The pupils of Stemster primary school on the occasion of the prize-giving, 2nd July, 1970. The school did not re-open after the summer holidays, and the pupils were transferred to Halkirk, Bower or Watten. The schools at Dunnet, Murkle, Janetstown and Spittal also closed that summer.

The presentation to John Dallas, retiring as headmaster of Miller Academy, Thurso in October, 1970.

B Company of the 51st Highland Volunteers parade at Wick station before embarking for the long journey to a training holiday in Malta, 24th July, 1970.

The Founder's Company of the Thurso Boys' Brigade on parade, 25th October, 1970.

Former-provost John Sinclair, Lord Lieutenant of Caithness, takes the salute during the Thurso Remembrance Day parade on 8th November, 1970.

Captain Malcolm Thomson of Stornoway visits Castletown primary school on 24th November, 1970 after his ship, a bulk carrier bound abroad, was put in touch with the school through the Ship Adoption Society.

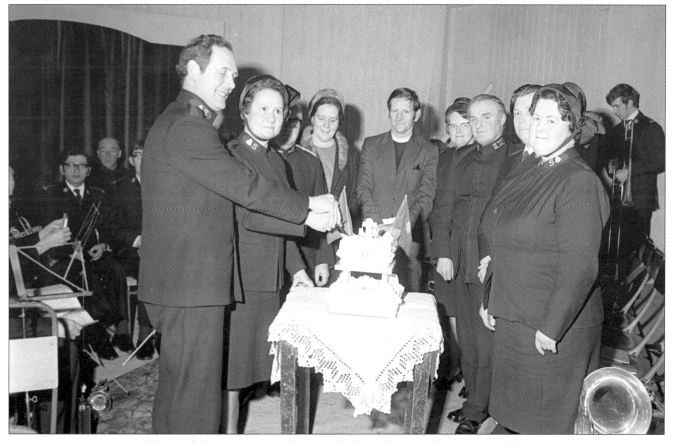

Thurso Salvation Army celebrates their anniversary, November, 1972.

Mr Morrison retires from the post of head teacher at Halkirk Primary School after 36 years, October 1972.

An unfortunate hair-do for this chiel on the eve of his wedding. Taken in Bank Row in 1971.
(Submitted by J. and W. Coghill, Watten. Copyright J. McDonald).

Thurso Fire Brigade are recognised as champions of the Northern Fire Area on 13th September, 1972. Thurso Provost Tom Pollock presented them with the efficiency shield and scroll, and the Stornoway Cup for winning the Northern Fire Area quiz.

The long arms of the law came in handy when men were needed to push this unexploded mine off Dunnet Beach, 24th May, 1968

141

Sponsored walk from Dunbeath to Wick, 25th May, 1968.

All set to go on the Darby and Joan Club outing, 28th May, 1968.

Wing Commander J. Hinchelwood inspects the Wick Air Training Corps.

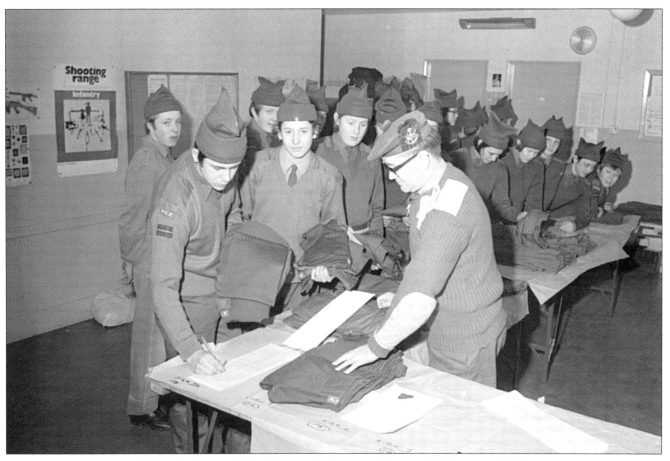

Thurso's Army Cadets inspect their new uniforms, 14th January, 1973.

Loads of fun at the Wick pre-school playgroup in March, 1970.

Liberal MP Cyril Smith after opening a sale of work in Thurso on 12th May, 1973.

A reception at Scapa House for Rear-Admiral David Dunbar-Naismith, Flag Officer Scotland and Northern Ireland, during a visit to HMS *Vulcan*.

The winners of the beard-growing competition sponsored by Lybster Portland FC in May 1973 - Jackie Hendry, Robin MacLeod and Sandy Robertson.

145

Wick Woolworths' staff at a function in the 1950s. (Submitted by M. Harrington, Thurso).

Dinner and dancing in the Seaview, John O'Groats in the sixties. (Submitted by M. Harrington, Thurso).

146

John Cormack, pictured in the late
1950s, outside his Bexley Terrace
fish and chip shop with customer,
Donald Wares. John died earlier
this year aged 98 years.
(Submitted by Z. Sinclair, Wick).

Wick Woolworths' staff pictured in the 1950s. (Submitted by M. Harrington, Thurso).

The Prince and Princess of Wales at Scrabster on 14th August, 1985, when the royal family landed from the *Britannia* to visit the Queen Mother at the Castle of Mey. (Submitted by M. Gunn, Halkirk).

In a joint exercise in Wick Bay on 7th September, 1973, an RAF helicopter from 202 Squadron, Lossiemouth, lifted men from the Wick lifeboat and from the seine-netter *Superb*.

Robert Cowe, the volunteer leader of the John O'Groats Rescue Company, receives the David Gunn Memorial Shield from Alex Rugg, convener of Caithness County Council, 22nd September, 1973.

The famous Wick Library crocodile enjoys an outing,
October, 1973.

Where are they now? The Wick pre-school playgroup, June 1974.

Spittal WRI celebrates its first birthday party, June 1974.

Lybster WRI celebrates its 43rd anniversary, September, 1975.

About 150 people crossed to Stroma in July 1975 to attend the dedication of the island's war memorial. The memorial was built by the Canisbay branch of the Royal British Legion and bears the names of twelve men who lost their lives in the two World Wars

Just the ticket? A get-together of bus conductresses in the Pentland Hotel, Thurso, November, 1977.

The conveners of the Wick Old Parish Church sale of work in 1975.
(Submitted by H. and M. Barrett, Thurso. Copyright J. McDonald).

Lyth WRI celebrate their 50th anniversary at the Seaview Hotel in November, 1977.

The sale of tickets for Concorde was an occasion for a celebration in the Wick British Airways office in June 1977.

Wick Brownies at the Rumster Forest Outdoor Centre, June 1977.

The staff at Bignold Hospital, Wick, get together to mark the retirement of matron, Miss May Sutherland, in May 1978.

Brownies and Guides from Wick at Thuster Farm, July 1978.

Bower Girl Guides, April 1978.

All dressed up for a concert in Bower hall, March, 1979.
(Submitted by C. Coghill, Georgemas).

On 14th March, 1980, James Callaghan, leader of the Labour Party, was guest of honour at the Canisbay Labour Party's annual dinner dance at the Seaview Hotel, John O'Groats.

Lesley Durrans, Thurso, won the Liza Keith Memorial Trophy at the local Mod on 31st May, 1986.

A get-together in 1986 to mark a visit from Thurso's twin town, Brilon in Germany.

Rev. Alistair Roy examines the
monument to the battle fought at
Altimarlach on 13th July, 1680.
The Wick Quatercentenary Committee
expressed interest in October, 1987 in
improving access to the Celtic cross
beside Wick River.

Television personality, Noel Edmonds, places a long-distance call from John O'Groats after opening the new digital exchange on 26th June, 1987.

Denny Miller, brewer, Jimmy Sinclair, mashman and Micky Miller, stillman, clocked up 95 years service between them in Pulteney Distillery by April, 1987.

Regional archaeologist, Rob Gourlay, examines a 4,000-year-old Bronze Age stone cist with a skeleton uncovered at Achavanich by William and Graham Ganson of Occumster in February, 1987.

The controversy over forestry planting in the Flow Country brought botanist and television personality Dr David Bellamy, to the north in February, 1988.

Sitka spruce planted on deep peat at Altnabreac, pictured in October, 1990.

Trade union officials and politicians got together at the Viewfirth Club, Thurso, to lead a public meeting in August, 1988 to protect against the government decision to phase out the fast reactor programme at Dounreay.

Two Wick High School teachers, Eric Farquhar and Phil Ward, relive the joys of boyhood during an exhibition of D.C. Thomson comics *The Dandy* and *The Beano* at the St. Fergus Gallery in August, 1988.

24th June, 1988 was the last day for the three pupils and the headmaster, David Jenkinson, of Altnabreac Primary School. Come August, the trio would begin to attend Halkirk Primary School, 16 miles away.

Wick farrier, Don Sutherland, was joined in the family firm in 1988 by his son, James (right) and Leslie Sutherland (no relation) when both qualified from Hereford Technical College.

A scene from Halkirk Drama Club's production of the comedy *Spreading the News* by Lady Gregory in the Scottish Community Drama Association district final in Thurso High School on 26-27th February, 1988.

The cast of the Wick Players production of *And So to Bed* by J. B. Fagan, performed in the Rifle Hall on 27 - 29th March, 1946. Tickets cost from sixpence to 5 shillings, and proceeds went to the Welcome Home and War Service Remembrance Fund. The *Groat* thought the play was 'brilliantly presented'.
From left: Neil Sutherland, Dolly Oag, John Ross, Mrs Jena Gordon, Bob Finlayson, Margaret Brokenshaw, Norman Halkett, Janet Black, Willie Magdelane, Margaret Sinclair, David Sutherland, Mrs Stella Roxburgh, Charlie Fraser, Rona Gray, George Tait, Jenny Barnie.
(Submitted by R. Taylor, Wick).

The Thurso Girls Brigade marching teams that won the British championship in Glasgow on 19th April, 1975. It was the first time the girls had entered the competition. Half of them had never been to a big city before and at least one of the group, unfazed by show business, found the most memorable part of the trip to be the first-time shopping in Sauchiehall Street. (Submitted by K. Coghill, Halkirk, copyright: M. Luciani).

Banniskirk WRI entertains Staxigoe WRI at the Ross Institute, Halkirk in the late 1940s.
(Submitted by W.S. Gunn, Hoy, Halkirk)

In the late 1940s Halkirk Players celebrated the arrival of midsummer with a night climb up Morven. (Submitted by W. Sutherland, Thurso).

George Gunn, playwright and founder of the Grey Coast Theatre Company, and Mairi MacIver of Eden Court Theatre examine stories of the Kildonan gold rush in old files of the Groat, to coincide with the première and tour of George's play *Gold* in September-October, 1989.

In Wick Town Hall on 12th December, 1989, Mrs Jess Campbell received a dinner set on the occasion of her retirement as depute chief executive of Caithness District Council.

Caithness folk get everywhere! Wick man, Thomas Sutherland, shakes the hand of an East German officer through a hole in the Berlin Wall, December, 1989.

Donald Omand, editor of *The New Caithness Book* published in December 1989 by North of Scotland Newspapers, signs copies in D.R. Simpson's bookshop.

Irish singer, Brendan Shine, ensured that 12th April, 1989 would be a day to remember for Helen Latimer from Thurso who was resident in the Queen Elizabeth wing of the Caithness General Hospital. The 12th was Mrs Latimer's 77th birthday. Also in the picture is Staff Nurse Sheena Kendrick.

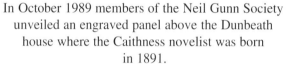

In October 1989 members of the Neil Gunn Society unveiled an engraved panel above the Dunbeath house where the Caithness novelist was born in 1891.

Jocky Begg and Jim Crowden with the human bones, possibly of Viking vintage, which they discovered while excavating ground for a new industrial estate at John O'Groats in February, 1989.

Keith Banks of Wick with a rare visitor, a hooptoe that stayed near the coastgard station for a short while in the autumn of 1989.

The banner of the men's Christian organisation known as the Brotherhood, was found in the Bridge Street Church early in 1989. Formed after the First World War, the Brotherhood had a large membership in Wick.

Mrs Annie Scott, born in County Tyrone, celebrated her 108th birthday and her ninth telegram from the Queen on 15th March, 1991. Mrs Scott lived in Achvarasdal.

It's 1987 and, at her retirement presentation, Mina Mackay can sit down at last after almost forty years service in the Ulbster Arms, Halkirk. Left to right: Keith Dreaves, Jessie Keith, Lord and Lady Thurso and Miranda Craigie. (Submitted by J. P. Campbell, Halkirk).

Elections and politicians

In May 1928, with a General Election approaching, Sir Archibald Sinclair MP pays a visit to Labour Party stalwart, George Green (fourth left), during the tattie planting at John O'Groats.
(Submitted by K. Green, John O'Groats).

A time when 'Petticoat government' came to Wick. The Kirking of the Provost, in this instance Miss Bessie Leith, who was elected to the position in 1949 after being a town councillor for three years. With her is Wick's first full-time town clerk, Miss Jess Page (later Mrs Campbell), who was also possibly Scotland's first female town clerk.
(Submitted by H. and M. Barrett, Thurso).

Billy Wolfe, chairman of the Scottish National Party, visits Wick fish market with local candidate Donald Barr during the 1970 General Election campaign. (Submitted by Z. Sinclair, Wick).

John Young, prospective Conservative candidate, at a daffodil tea in the Station Hotel, Wick, on 18th April, 1970.

Castletown branch of the Labour Party gearing up for the campaign to re-elect Robert Maclennan in the General Election, June 1970.

Willie Ross, Secretary of State for Scotland, visits the Scottish Instruments factory at Wick on 3rd June, 1970.

Staff in the Leather Factory, Wick, receive a visit from David Steel, then a Liberal MP and his Party's chief whip, on 10th January, 1973.

Prime Minister Ted Heath visited Wick on 10th September, 1973.

Roxanne Macleod presents a gift to Shadow Scottish Secretary Donald Dewar after he opened the Wick Labour Party's sale of work in October, 1988. Roxanne's uncle John Macleod looks on.

Mining engineer Paul Gillon (left) and Alex Salmond MP, then the SNP's energy spokesman, visited Wick to talk to a meeting organised by CAND (Caithness Against Nuclear Dumping) in February 1989 in relation to the proposal by NIREX to explore Caithness for a site for a potential nuclear waste depository.
CAND vice-convener John Bogle is in the centre.

George Bruce, prospective Conservative candidate for Caithness and Sutherland, has a surprise encounter with Prime Minister John Major at the Lybster Gala in August, 1991.

Ready for a new decade – the annual dinner of Caithness Chamber of Commerce in 1991, with guest speakers Robert Maclennan MP and the Lord Chancellor, Lord Mackay of Clashfern (second and third from left in front row). Back, left to right: J. Innes, D. Hanson, G. Bruce, B. Brock, G. Gibson, D. Coghill. Front: H. Kennedy, R. Maclennan, Lord Mackay of Clashfern (Lord Chancellor), Lord Thurso, Mrs M. Richard.(Submitted by C. Richard, Broadhaven).

A gallery from the past

Studio portraits: Left to right: Humphrey, Wick, Swanson, Thurso, John B. Russell, Thurso and Alec Johnston, Wick.

This family photograph is of William and Margaret Thain and their family who, as far as we know, lived at 8 Shore Houses, Ackergill. William Thain was coxswain of the Ackergill lifeboat from 1878 to 1894. His son, James Thain, was coxswain from 1913 to 1930. (Submitted by Margaret Hammerton).

Jimmy Nicol, chauffeur to Lord Horne of Stirkoke House. Pictured with his gleaming charge. (Submitted by Margaret Hammerton).

Wick Brownies Easter Bonnet competition, 1976.

Wick Bridge Street Youth Club table tennis practice match.

Prizewinners of the Thurso Amateur Wrestling championships, Royal British Legion Club, Thurso, 1970.

Wick High School 1970, winners of the North of Scotland Milk Marketing Board's Art competition receive their prizes from William Ronaldson, Westerseat with Principal Art Teacher James Leishman, on the left, and Rector John Ross, pictured right.

Liberal leader Jeremy Thorpe addresses a captive audience at Thurso Town Hall in May, 1970.

Sir Alec Douglas-Home (Conservative leader), meets the folk at Pulteney House, Wick in 1970.

The Quatercentenary Committee that met to oversee Wick's 400th anniversary of the awarding of Royal Burgh status by James VI in 1589.

The ruins of Buchollie Castle on its dramatic sea stack at Freswick.